ABOUT THIS BOOK

The photographs for this book were taken in Canada, Italy, Kenya, and the United States of America using Leica and Canon cameras to capture the superpowers of the dogs pictured here. This book was edited by Lisa Yoskowitz and designed by Carla Weiss. The production was supervised by Dave Klimowicz, and the production editor was Marisa Finkelstein. The text was set in Avenir 55 Roman, and the display type is Detroit 05 Base.

Little, Brown and Company
Hachette Book Group
1290 Avenue of the Americas, New York, NY 10104
Visit us at LBYR.com

First Edition: March 2019

Little, Brown and Company is a division of Hachette Book Group, Inc.
The Little, Brown name and logo are trademarks of Hachette Book Group, Inc.

The publisher is not responsible for websites (or their content) that are not owned by the publisher.

Library of Congress Control Number: 2018957883

ISBNs: 978-0-316-45359-2 (hardcover), 978-0-316-45358-5 (ebook), 978-0-316-45354-7 (ebook), 978-0-316-45355-4 (ebook)

PRINTED IN CHINA

1010

10 9 8 7 6 5 4 3 2 1

SUPERPOWER DOGS

By Taran, George, Daniel, and Dominic

Photographs by Danny Wilcox Frazier

LITTLE, BROWN AND COMPANY

New York   Boston

These are the stories of some of the world's most amazing superheroes.

★

These dogs and their human partners work together to save lives, fight crime, and help people heal.

HALO

is training to become an
Urban Search and Rescue dog.

HALO
lives in
Miami, Florida,
USA.

Human partner: **CAT**

Fire captain Cat Labrada has made it her mission to train dogs to save lives. Cat has raised Halo since she was a puppy.

Halo is learning how to find and rescue people who need help after earthquakes and other disasters.

Captain Cat teaches Halo how to follow directions, ignore tempting distractions like food and toys, and focus on finding people by smell.

HALO'S NIGHT VISION is five times better than yours, and she can see the slightest movement from a mile away! Her amazing hearing can pick up faraway cries for help and figure out where they are coming from in a fraction of a second.

Before Halo can join Cat's K9 unit, she has to take a big test. She studies for it in Disaster City, Texas. If she does well, she'll join the ranks of many other amazing Superpower Dogs....

HENRY

is an avalanche rescue dog who is small
enough to ride on his human partner's shoulders.
His size also allows him to skip over deep snow
without sinking down into it.

AN AVALANCHE IS A DANGEROUS EVENT where a large amount of snow, ice, and sometimes rocks quickly slide down a mountain. Avalanches are hazardous to people who get caught in their path, so it's important to be safe on snowy mountains and pay attention to any warnings in the area.

HENRY lives in Whistler, British Columbia, Canada.

Human partner: **IAN**

Henry often arrives at the scene of an avalanche with Ian. They'll race there on skis, chairlifts, or snowmobiles; by foot and paw; or even by being lowered from a helicopter!

Once he's on the scene, Henry runs across the snow, sniffing as he goes. Henry can find someone lost in the snow in less time than people or machines can. He can smell a person trapped under many feet of snow.

A LOT OF DIFFERENT BREEDS make great avalanche rescue dogs, including golden retrievers, German shepherds, Labrador retrievers, and border collies like Henry. It takes about a year of training to become an official avalanche rescue dog.

After Henry catches
a scent, he'll bark,
scratch, and dig his
way to the rescue.

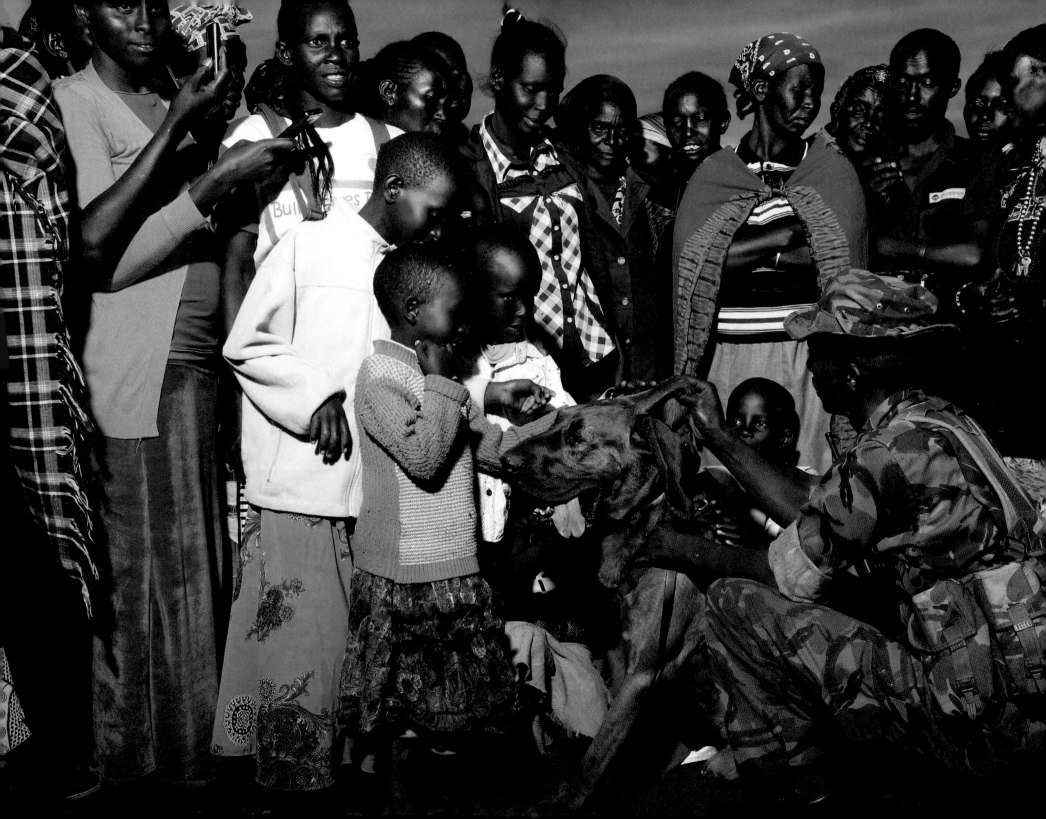

TIPPER AND TONY

are bloodhound brothers
who are loved by an entire community
for their work in helping to keep
other animals safe.

SENSE OF SMELL

is the bloodhound's ultimate superpower. Their noses pick up on people's sweat, breath, skin, and bacteria. Many types of dogs are able to find or trace a person they're looking for by following an invisible trail of smells. Bloodhounds are the best trackers in the dog kingdom.

TIPPER AND TONY live in Lewa Wildlife Conservancy, Isiolo, Kenya.

Human partners:
ELOISE, JOSEPH OF THE LEWA CONSERVANCY DOG UNIT, AND THE KENYA WILDLIFE SERVICE

Born and raised in Kenya, Tipper and Tony have been trained to protect the wildlife there, including many endangered species.

WHEN A CERTAIN TYPE of animal is harder and harder to find in the wild, an animal becomes "endangered." Endangered animals are given special protections to help keep them safe. Poachers are people who hunt animals illegally.

An entire team of park rangers protects and supports Tipper and Tony. The dogs' work is very important: they track poachers who are trying to hurt endangered animals. They can pick up a smell that's days old and follow that smell all the way to the poacher who left it.

Tipper and Tony have led their human partners to make over forty arrests! Many giraffes, elephants, zebras, lions, and rhinos have been saved by these amazing dogs.

RICOCHET

is a surfing dog. She also has the
ability to sense people's emotions.

RICOCHET
lives in
San Diego,
California,
USA.

Human partner: **JUDY**

Ricochet surfs with people who need help to feel calm and happy, from young kids to soldiers who have returned from duty.

REEF

is a natural-born lifeguard.
She works on behalf of the Italian
coast guard's K9 team.

REEF IS A NEWFOUNDLAND,
a breed with waterproof fur,
webbed paws, strong muscles,
and a body perfectly shaped
for swimming. These dogs can
swim huge distances without
tiring. They are perfect
for water rescues.

REEF
lives near
Milan, Italy.

Human partner: FERRUCCIO

Reef uses her rescue instincts and skills to find people lost in the water and bring rescuers to them—or even tow them to shore herself. One dog like Reef can pull six people through the water!

AS MANY AS FOUR HUNDRED water rescue dogs work in Italy alone!

Reef has saved many lives, and now she helps teach other dogs how to carry out water rescues.

Not every dog is meant to fight crime or save lives, but all dogs have superpowers.

They can give unconditional love, keep you safe,
find you when you're lost, or make you feel better
when you're sad.

SUPERPOWER BREEDS

There are many different kinds of working dogs who can do many different jobs. Here are just a few breeds that you might find hard at work, as well as some of their typical superpowers. Remember, every dog is unique, and every dog has amazing abilities!

★ BELGIAN MALINOIS ★

PERSONALITY
✓Intelligent ✓Friendly ✓Energetic
✓Hardworking

SUPERPOWERS
✓Easy to train because they love working (especially when treats are involved!)

IDEAL JOBS
✓Search and rescue ✓Service

★ BLOODHOUND ★

PERSONALITY
✓Inquisitive ✓Patient ✓Independent
✓Friendly

SUPERPOWERS
✓The top dogs in scent detection, they won't give up until they find their target

IDEAL JOBS
✓Tracking criminals and lost or missing people

★ BORDER COLLIE ★

PERSONALITY
✓Focused ✓Highly intelligent
✓Energetic

SUPERPOWERS
✓Incredibly agile
✓Great at scenting the air

IDEAL JOBS
✓Herding ✓Search and rescue

★ DUTCH SHEPHERD ★

PERSONALITY
✓Loyal ✓Intelligent ✓Curious
✓Agile ✓Independent ✓Eager

SUPERPOWERS
✓Tireless (they can run all day long!)
✓Amazing scent-detecting and tracking skills

IDEAL JOBS
✓Herding ✓Search and rescue
✓Police and military work

★ GERMAN SHEPHERD ★

PERSONALITY
✓Loyal ✓Courageous ✓Confident
✓Hardworking ✓Highly intelligent

SUPERPOWERS
✓Fearless fighters and extremely trainable, they make ideal police and guard dogs

IDEAL JOBS
✓Search and rescue ✓Service
✓Police and military work

★ GOLDEN RETRIEVER ★

PERSONALITY
✓Friendly ✓Obedient ✓Smart
✓Outgoing ✓Loyal

SUPERPOWERS
✓Good hunting dogs ✓Excellent swimmers ✓Great companions

IDEAL JOBS
✓Search and rescue ✓Emotional therapy ✓Service

★ LABRADOR RETRIEVER ★

PERSONALITY
✓Playful ✓Respectful ✓Dedicated
✓Smart ✓Easygoing

SUPERPOWERS
✓Incredibly athletic and skilled at swimming, these dogs are also known for being extra social and loving

IDEAL JOBS
✓Search and rescue ✓Emotional therapy ✓Service

★ NEWFOUNDLAND ★

PERSONALITY
✓Sweet-tempered ✓Loyal ✓Gentle

SUPERPOWERS
✓Excellent swimmers
✓Big and strong

IDEAL JOBS
✓Water rescues

★ SAINT BERNARD ★

PERSONALITY
✓Patient ✓Fun-loving ✓Loyal

SUPERPOWERS
✓Strong enough to pull small carts
✓Powerful sense of smell

IDEAL JOBS
✓Once a search and rescue breed, now primarily a family companion

★ SIBERIAN HUSKY ★

PERSONALITY
✓Loyal ✓Friendly ✓Outgoing
✓Highly intelligent

SUPERPOWERS
✓Incredible endurance ✓Ability to withstand subzero temperatures for long periods of time

IDEAL JOBS
✓Search and rescue, particularly avalanche recovery

SUPERPOWER DOGS IN ACTION

These dogs are hard at work (or play!). The authors invite dog owners to visit superpowerdogs.com to share their dog's superpowers.

BEHIND THE SUPERPOWER SCENES

The photos in this book were captured during the filming of *Superpower Dogs,* an immersive **IMAX**® adventure that presents the inspiring true story of the world's most extraordinary dogs and the remarkable science behind their lifesaving superpowers. Here's a look behind the scenes:

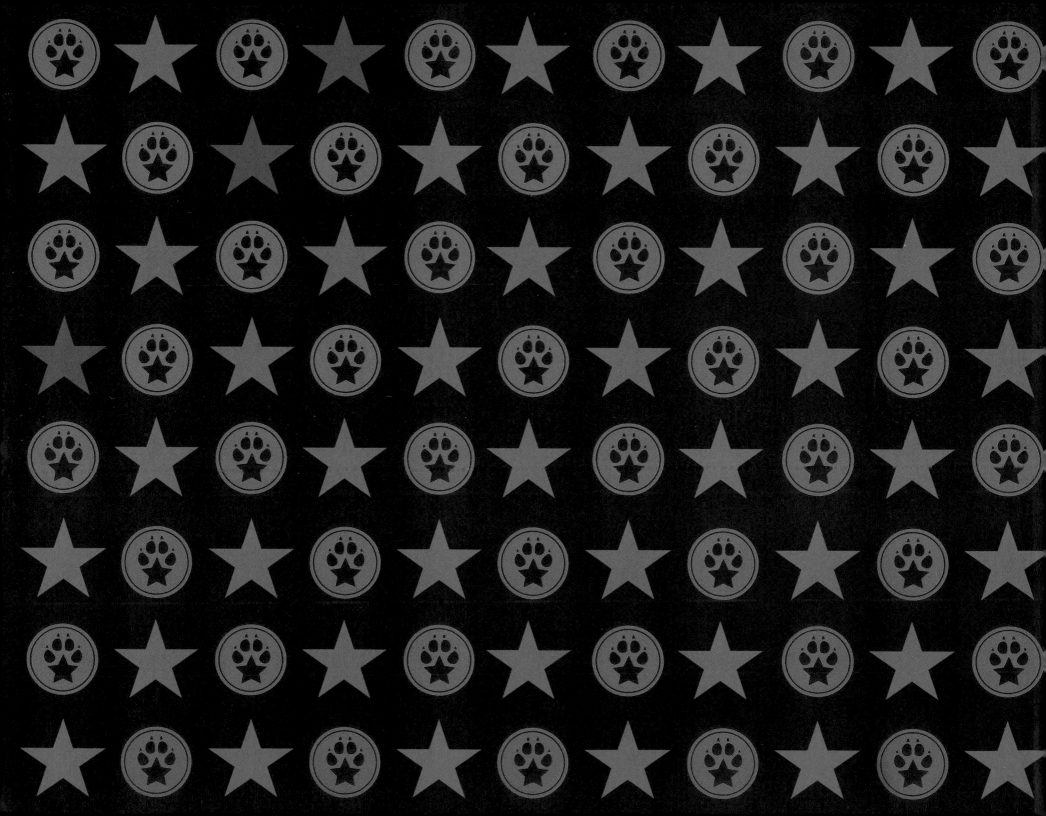